Table of contents

T0357284

Exercise 2.1
Valley Enterprises P/L

Cash Count

Denomination	Count	Value
Date:		
$100.00	5	
50.00	35	
20.00	25	
10.00	21	
5.00	95	
2.00	37	
1.00	75	
0.50	39	
0.20	143	
0.10	15	
0.05	8	
TOTAL CASH		

Credit Cards

	Date:	
Visa Cards Received		$25.50
		$2,060.00
		$38.00
		$235.60
Visa Card Credits		
TOTAL VISA CARD:		
Mastercards Received		$101.95
		$73.00
		$1,044.00
		$217.00
Mastercard Credits		-$100.00
TOTAL MASTERCARD:		

CHEQUES

Dated	Drawer	Bank	Branch	Amount
April 23	F. Salerno	CBC	Carlton	$1,206.40
April 24	L. Buchari	WBC	Cromer	$195.00
April 24	G. Kao	NAB	Upfield	$142.95
April 25	L. Chan	CBA	Glen Alvi	$73.00
			TOTAL	

FINAL TILL RECEIPT
25 April 20CY
1835 HRS

Dept_001	2,645.70
Dept_002	4,801.30
Dept_003	824.40
Dept_004	675.00
DEPT TOTALS	**8,946.40**
Cash	3,634.00
Cheques	1,617.35
Visa	2,359.10
Master	1,335.95
Subtotal	8,946.40
Cash out (PTO for details)	0.00
TOTAL	**8946.4**

Exercise 2.1 (continued)

Valley Enterprises P/L

DAILY TAKINGS RECONCILIATION		
DATE:		
SALES		
Plants (Dept 1)		
Pots (Dept 2)		
Fertilisers (Dept 3)		
Pesticides (Dept 4)		
TOTAL SALES		
MADE UP BY		
Denomination		
Notes	$100	
	50	
	20	
	10	
	5	
TOTAL NOTES		
Coins	$2	
	1	
	0.50	
	0.20	
	0.10	
	0.05	
TOTAL COINS		
Cheques		
Credit Cards	Visa	
	Master	
TOTAL CREDIT CARDS		
GRAND TOTAL		
Completed by:		
Checked by supervisor:		

Exercise 2.2

			Cash Receipts					
Date	Rec No.	Received From	Sales	GST collected	General	GST Free Sales	Bank	

Exercise 2.3

			Cash Payment					
Date	Chq No.	Paid to For	Purchases	GST Paid	General	GST Free Purchases	Bank	

Exercise 2.4 and 2.5

	Rec			GST		GST Free		
Date	No.		Sales	collected	General	Sales	✓	Bank
1/3/CY								

Cash Receipts

	Chq					GST Free		
Date	No.		Purchases	GST Paid	General	Purchases	✓	Bank
1/3/CY								

Cash Payments

Exercise 2.6

Abel Co. Bank Reconciliation For March 20CY	
Closing Credit Balance Bank Statement	$
Plus Outstanding Deposit	+
Subtotal	
Minus Unpresented Cheque	-
Equals Cashbook Debit Balance	

Scenario 2.1 and 2.2

Smart Co

Smart Co Bank Reconciliation For January 20CY		
Closing Credit Balance Bank Statement	$	2,390.00
Plus Outstanding Deposit	+	1,750.00
Subtotal		4,140.00
Minus Unpresented Cheque		
Chq177	$1,090.00	
	-	1,090.00
Equals Cashbook Debit Balance		3,050.00

Cash Receipts								
Date	Rec No.	Received From	Sales	GST collected	General	GST Free Sales	✓	Bank

Cash Payments								
Date	Chq No.	Paid to For	Purchases	GST Paid	General	GST Free Purchases	✓	Bank

Scenario 2.1 and 2.2 (continued)

Smart Co

Smart Co Bank Reconciliation For February 20CY				
Closing Debit Balance Bank Statement			$	820.55
Plus Unpresented Cheque				
	Chq	4186	341.00	
	Chq	4187	1,314.50 +	1,655.50
Subtotal				2,476.05
Minus Outstanding Deposit				
			-	2,310.00
Equals Cashbook Debit Balance				166.05

Cash Receipts								
Date	Rec No.	Received From	Sales	GST collected	General	GST Free Sales	✓	Bank

Scenario 2.1 and 2.2 (continued)

Smart Co

							GST Free		
Date	**Chq No.**	**Paid to For**	Purchases	**GST Paid**	**General**		**Purchases**	✓	**Bank**

Smart Co Bank Reconciliation For March 20CY		
Closing Credit Balance Bank Statement	$	
Plus Outstanding Deposit	+	
Subtotal		
Minus Unpresented Cheque		
Chq		
Chq		
Chq		
Chq		
	-	
Equals Cashbook Debit Balance		

Exercise 2.7

Abel Co.

Petty Cash Voucher			
Date:			001
Debit:			
Particulars			
Details	Acquisitns	GST	Total
		TOTAL:	
Received:		Approved:	

Petty Cash Voucher			
Date:			002
Debit:			
Particulars			
Details	Acquisitns	GST	Total
		TOTAL:	
Received:		Approved:	

Petty Cash Voucher			
Date:			003
Debit:			
Particulars			
Details	Acquisitns	GST	Total
		TOTAL:	
Received:		Approved:	

Petty Cash Voucher			
Date:			004
Debit:			
Particulars			
Details	Acquisitns	GST	Total
		TOTAL:	
Received:		Approved:	

Petty Cash Voucher			
Date:			005
Debit:			
Particulars			
Details	Acquisitns	GST	Total
		TOTAL:	
Received:		Approved:	

Petty Cash Voucher			
Date:			006
Debit:			
Particulars			
Details	Acquisitns	GST	Total
		TOTAL:	
Received:		Approved:	

Exercise 2.7 (continued)

Abel Co.

				Voucher				
Amount Received	Date	Details	No.	Total	GST Paid	Travel	Office	Sundries

Petty Cash Book

CHEQUE REQUISITION

REQUESTER INFORMATION

Name: _____   Ext: _____

Dept: _____   Date: _____

VENDOR INFORMATION

Name on
Cheque
Address: _____

_____

_____

PAYMENT DESCRIPTION

Reason for Cheque	Account	Amount
Cheque total:		

Signed: _____   Authorised: _____

Scenario 2.3

Smart Co.

Petty Cash Voucher			
Date:			001
Debit:			
Particulars			
Details	Acquisitns	GST	Total
		TOTAL:	
Received:		**Approved:**	

Petty Cash Voucher			
Date:			002
Debit:			
Particulars			
Details	Acquisitns	GST	Total
		TOTAL:	
Received:		**Approved:**	

Petty Cash Voucher			
Date:			003
Debit:			
Particulars			
Details	Acquisitns	GST	Total
		TOTAL:	
Received:		**Approved:**	

Petty Cash Voucher			
Date:			004
Debit:			
Particulars			
Details	Acquisitns	GST	Total
		TOTAL:	
Received:		**Approved:**	

Petty Cash Voucher			
Date:			005
Debit:			
Particulars			
Details	Acquisitns	GST	Total
		TOTAL:	
Received:		**Approved:**	

Petty Cash Voucher			
Date:			006
Debit:			
Particulars			
Details	Acquisitns	GST	Total
		TOTAL:	
Received:		**Approved:**	

Petty Cash Voucher			
Date:			007
Debit:			
Particulars			
Details	Acquisitns	GST	Total
		TOTAL:	
Received:		**Approved:**	

Petty Cash Voucher			
Date:			008
Debit:			
Particulars			
Details	Acquisitns	GST	Total
		TOTAL:	
Received:		**Approved:**	

Scenario 2.3 (continued)

Smart Co.

Amnt Recvd	Date	Details	No.	Vouchr total	GST Paid	Trvel	Office Supps	Staff Amens	Motr Veh	Sundrs

Petty Cash Book

MEMO

From: Date:

To: Subject:

Scenario 2.3 (continued)

Smart Co.

CHEQUE REQUISITION		
REQUESTER INFORMATION		
Name: _____	**Ext:** _____	
Dept: _____	**Date:** _____	
VENDOR INFORMATION		
Name on Cheque _____		
Address: _____		
_____		
_____		
PAYMENT DESCRIPTION		
Reason for Cheque	**Account**	**Amount**
	Cheque total:	_____
Signed:	**Authorised:**	
	Chq No:	

Scenario 2.4

Smart Co.

Date	Details	✓	Rceipt Total		Purchs	GST Paid	Motor Veh	Office	Staff Amen	Sundrs
	TOTALS									

Date	Chq No.	Paid to or for	Purchases	GST Paid	General	GST Free Purchases	Bank

Exercise 3.1

Michael Pty Ltd

	General Journal				GJ1
Date	Particulars	Folio	Debit	Credit	

Cheque Account					1.10
Date	Particulars	Folio	Debit	Credit	Balance
						Dr

Accounts Receivable					1.12
Date	Particulars	Folio	Debit	Credit	Balance

Less Provision for doubtful debts					1.121
Date	Particulars	Folio	Debit	Credit	Balance

Inventory					1.13
Date	Particulars	Folio	Debit	Credit	Balance

Office Equipment at Cost					1.211
Date	Particulars	Folio	Debit	Credit	Balance

Exercise 3.1 (continued)

Michael Pty Ltd

Office Equip Accum Depn — 1.212

Date	Particulars	Folio	Debit	Credit	Balance

Van at Cost — 1.221

Date	Particulars	Folio	Debit	Credit	Balance

Van Accum Depn — 1.222

Date	Particulars	Folio	Debit	Credit	Balance

Visa Card — 2.114

Date	Particulars	Folio	Debit	Credit	Balance

Accounts Payable — 2.12

Date	Particulars	Folio	Debit	Credit	Balance

GST Collected — 2.131

Date	Particulars	Folio	Debit	Credit	Balance

GST Paid — 2.132

Date	Particulars	Folio	Debit	Credit	Balance

Owner's Capital — 3.11

Date	Particulars	Folio	Debit	Credit	Balance

Exercise 3.1 (continued)

Michael Pty Ltd

Owner drawings					3.12
Date	Particulars	Folio	Debit	Credit	Balance

Rent					6.25
Date	Particulars	Folio	Debit	Credit	Balance

Trial Balance to 31/01/20CY			
Accnt No.	Account Name	Debit	Credit
1.10	Cheque Account		
1.12	Accounts Receivable		
1.121	Less Prov'n Doubtful Debts		
1.13	Inventory		
1.211	Office Equip at Cost		
1.212	Office Equip Accum Depn		
1.221	Van at Cost		
1.222	Van Accum Depn		
2.114	Visa Card		
2.12	Accounts Payable		
2.131	GST Collected		
2.132	GST Paid		
3.11	Owner's Capital		
3.12	Owner Drawings		
6.25	Rent		
	TOTALS		

Scenario 3.1

Elite Co.

General Journal				GJ1
Date	Particulars	Folio	Debit	Credit

Cheque Account					1.10
Date	Particulars	Folio	Debit	Credit	Balance

High Interest Bank Account					1.113
Date	Particulars	Folio	Debit	Credit	Balance

Accounts Receivable					1.12
Date	Particulars	Folio	Debit	Credit	Balance

Less Prov'n for Doubtful Debts					1.121
Date	Particulars	Folio	Debit	Credit	Balance

Furniture and Fixtures at cost					1.311
Date	Particulars	Folio	Debit	Credit	Balance

Scenario 3.1 (continued)
Elite Co.

Furniture and Fixtures accum depn					1.312
Date	Particulars	Folio	Debit	Credit	Balance

Visa Card					2.114
Date	Particulars	Folio	Debit	Credit	Balance

Accounts Payable					2.12
Date	Particulars	Folio	Debit	Credit	Balance

GST Collected					2.131
Date	Particulars	Folio	Debit	Credit	Balance

GST Paid					2.132
Date	Particulars	Folio	Debit	Credit	Balance

Owner's Capital					3.11
Date	Particulars	Folio	Debit	Credit	Balance

Owner Drawings					3.12
Date	Particulars	Folio	Debit	Credit	Balance

Electricity					6.242
Date	Particulars	Folio	Debit	Credit	Balance

Scenario 3.1 (continued)

Elite Co.

Accnt No.	Account Name	Debit	Credit
1.10			
1.113			
1.12			
1.121			
1.311			
1.312			
2.114			
2.12			
2.131			
2.132			
3.11			
3.12			
6.242			
	TOTALS		

Trial Balance to 31/01/20CY

Exercise 3.2 and 3.3

Doug Co.

Purchase Journal						PJ1
Date	Inv No.	Particulars	Folio	Purchases	GST Paid	Acct Pay Total

Purchase Returns and Allowances						PR1
Date	Adj Note No.	Particulars	Folio	Purchase Returns	GST Paid Adj	Acct Pay Total

Cash Payments Journal										CP1
Date	Chq No.	Particulars	Folio	Discnt	GST Adj	Acct Pay	Prchases	GST Paid	General	Bank

Isawaki P/L				S 01
Date	Particulars	Debit	Credit	Balance

M Lee P/L				S 02
Date	Particulars	Debit	Credit	Balance

Malouf & Co				S 03
Date	Particulars	Debit	Credit	Balance

Exercise 3.2 and 3.3 (continued)

Doug Co.

Cheque Account 1.10

Date	Particulars	Folio	Debit	Credit	Balance
31/12	Balance brought forward		12,360.00		12,360.00

Accounts Payable 2.12

Date	Particulars	Folio	Debit	Credit	Balance

GST Paid 2.132

Date	Particulars	Folio	Debit	Credit	Balance

Owner Capital 3.10

Date	Particulars	Folio	Debit	Credit	Balance
31/12	Balance brought forward			12,360.00	12,360.00

Discount Received 4.90

Date	Particulars	Folio	Debit	Credit	Balance

Hardware Purchases 5.10

Date	Particulars	Folio	Debit	Credit	Balance

Purchase Returns and Allowances 5.20

Date	Particulars	Folio	Debit	Credit	Balance

Telephone 6.46

Date	Particulars	Folio	Debit	Credit	Balance

Exercise 3.2 and 3.3 (continued)

Doug Co.

3.2 AFTER PURCHASES JOURNAL

Schedule of Accounts Payable as at 31/1/20CY		
Accnt No.	Account Name	Balance Owed
	TOTALS	

Trial Balance to 31/01/20CY			
Accnt No.	Account Name	Debit	Credit
	TOTALS		

3.2 AFTER PURCHASES RETURNS AND CASH PAYMENTS

Schedule of Accounts Payable as at 31/1/20CY		
Accnt No.	Account Name	Balance Owed
	TOTALS	

Trial Balance to 31/01/20CY			
Accnt No.	Account Name	Debit	Credit
	TOTALS		

Scenario 3.2

Elite Co.

Purchase Journal — PJ1

Date	Inv No.	Particulars	Folio	Purchases	GST Paid	Acct Pay Total

Purchase Returns and Allowances — PR1

Date	Adj Note No.	Particulars	Folio	Purchase Returns	GST Paid Adj	Acct Pay Total

Cash Payments Journal — CP1

Date	Chq No.	Particulars	Folio	Discnt	GST Adj	Acct Pay	Prchses	GST Paid	General	Bank

Bui & Co — S 01

Date	Particulars	Debit	Credit	Balance	
					Cr
					Cr
					Cr
					Cr
					Cr
					Cr
					Cr

S Ahuja — S 02

Date	Particulars	Debit	Credit	Balance	
					Cr
					Cr
					Cr

Scenario 3.2 (continued)

Elite Co.

Cheok & Son					S 03	
Date	Particulars	Debit	Credit	Balance		
14/2	Purchases (Inv 2211)		1,980.00	1,980.00	Cr	
20/2	Purchases (Inv 2231)		3,168.00	5,148.00	Cr	
					Cr	
					Cr	
					Cr	

Eriser P/L					S 04	
Date	Particulars	Debit	Credit	Balance		
					Cr	
					Cr	
					Cr	

Citipower					S 05	
Date	Particulars	Debit	Credit	Balance		
2/3	Electicity		583.00	583.00	Cr	

The accounts general ledger can be found on a separate
page labelled Elite General Ledger starting on page 33.

Schedule of Accounts Payable as at 31/3/20CY		
Accnt No.	Account Name	Balance Owed
S 01	Bui & Co	
S 02	S Ahuja	
S 03	Cheok & Son	
S 04	Eriser P/L	
S 05	Citipower	
	TOTALS	

Scenario 3.2 (continued)

Elite Co.

Accnt No.	Account Name	Debit	Credit
1.10	Cheque Account		
1.113	High Interest Account		
1.12	Accounts Receivable		
1.121	Less Prov'n Doubtful Debts		
1.311	Furniture and Fixtures at Cost		
1.312	Furniture and Fixtures Accum Depn		
2.114	Visa Card		
2.12	Accounts Payable		
2.131	GST Collected		
2.132	GST Paid		
3.11	Owner's Capital		
3.12	Owner Drawings		
4.90	Discounts Received		
5.11	Goldware Purchases		
5.12	Purchase of Consumables		
5.20	Purchase Returns		
6.18	Office Supplies		
6.242	Electricity		
	TOTALS		

Trial Balance to 31/03/20CY

Exercise 3.4 and 3.5

Paul Co.

Sales Journal							SJ1
Date	Inv No.	Particulars	Folio	Sales	GST Collected	Acc Rec Total	

Sales Returns and Allowances						SR1
Date	Adj Note No.	Particulars	Folio	Sales Returns	GST Collctd Adj	Acc Rec Adjust

Cash Receipts Journal									CR1
Date	Rcpt	Particulars	Folio	Discnt	GST Adj	Acct Rec	Sales	GST Collctd	General	Bank

V Lau				C 01	
Date	Particulars	Debit	Credit	Balance	
					Dr
					Dr
					Dr
					Dr

L Singh				C 02	
Date	Particulars	Debit	Credit	Balance	
					Dr
					Dr

M Viney				C 03	
Date	Particulars	Debit	Credit	Balance	
					Dr
					Dr
					Dr
					Dr

Exercise 3.4 and 3.5 (continued)

Paul Co.

Cheque Account						1.10
Date	Particulars	Folio	Debit	Credit		Balance
31/12	Balance brought forward		10,000.00			10,000.00

Accounts Receivable						1.12
Date	Particulars	Folio	Debit	Credit		Balance

GST Collected						2.131
Date	Particulars	Folio	Debit	Credit		Balance

Owner Capital						3.1
Date	Particulars	Folio	Debit	Credit		Balance
31/12	Balance brought forward			10,000.00		10,000.00

Sales						4.1
Date	Particulars	Folio	Debit	Credit		Balance

Sales Returns and Allowances						4.2
Date	Particulars	Folio	Debit	Credit		Balance

Discounts Given						5.9
Date	Particulars	Folio	Debit	Credit		Balance

Interest Income						8.10
Date	Particulars	Folio	Debit	Credit		Balance

Exercise 3.4 and 3.5 (continued)

Paul Co.

3.4 AFTER SALES JOURNAL

Schedule of Accounts Receivable as at 31/1/20CY		
Accnt No.	Account Name	Balance Owed
	TOTALS	

Trial Balance to 31/01/20CY			
Accnt No.	Account Name	Debit	Credit
	TOTALS		

3.5 AFTER SALES RETURNS AND CASH RECEIPTS

Schedule of Accounts Receivable as at 31/1/20CY		
Accnt No.	Account Name	Balance Owed
	TOTALS	

Trial Balance to 31/01/20CY			
Accnt No.	Account Name	Debit	Credit
	TOTALS		

Scenario 3.3 to 3.5
Elite Co.

Sales Journal						SJ1
Date	Inv No.	Particulars	Folio	Sales	GST Collected	Acc Rec Total

Sales Returns and Allowances						SR1
Date	Adj Note No.	Particulars	Folio	Sales Returns	GST Collctd Adj	Acc Rec Adjust

Cash Receipts Journal											CR1
Date	Rcpt	Particulars	Folio	Discnt	GST Adj	Acct Rec	Sales	GST Coll	General	Bank	

Touma P/L				C 01
Date	Particulars	Debit	Credit	Balance

V Maris				C 02
Date	Particulars	Debit	Credit	Balance

Scenario 3.3 to 3.5 (continued)

Elite Co.

Y Yao   C 03

Date	Particulars	Debit	Credit	Balance	
					Dr
					Dr
					Dr
					Dr
					Dr
					Dr

A Wilson   C 04

Date	Particulars	Debit	Credit	Balance	
					Dr
					Dr

J Dawe   C 05

Date	Particulars	Debit	Credit	Balance	
1/2	Sales (Inv 106)	411.40		411.40	Dr
15/2	Sales (Inv 107)	165.00		576.40	Dr

V Maris - Supplier   S 06

Date	Particulars	Debit	Credit	Balance	
					Cr
					Cr

**The accounts general ledger can be found on a separate
page labelled Elite General Ledger starting at page 33**

	General Journal			GJ1
Date	Particulars	Folio	Debit	Credit

Scenario 3.3 to 3.5 (continued)

Elite Co.

3.3 After Sales, Returns and Receipts posted

Schedule of Accounts Receivable as at 31/3/20CY		
Accnt No.	Account Name	Balance Owed
C 01	Touma P/L	
C 02	V Maris	
C 03	Y Yao	
C 04	A Wilson	
C 05	J Dawe	
	TOTALS	

Trial Balance to 31/03/20CY			
Accnt No.	Account Name	Debit	Credit
1.10	Cheque Account		
1.113	High Interest Account		
1.12	Accounts Receivable		
1.121	Less Prov'n Doubtful Debts		
1.311	Furniture and Fixtures at Cost		
1.312	Furniture and Fixtures Accum Depn		
2.114	Visa Card		
2.12	Accounts Payable		
2.131	GST Collected		
2.132	GST Paid		
3.11	Owner's Capital		
3.12	Owner Drawings		
4.11	Goldware Sales		
4.12	Jewellery Evaluations		
4.20	Sales Returns		
4.90	Discounts Received		
5.11	Goldware Purchases		
5.12	Purchase of Consumables		
5.20	Purchase Returns		
5.90	Discounts Given		
6.18	Office Supplies		
6.242	Electricity		
8.1	Interest Income		
	TOTALS		

Scenario 3.3 to 3.5 (continued)
Elite Co.

3.4 After bad debt posted

	Schedule of Accounts Receivable as at 31/3/20CY		
Accnt No.	Account Name		Balance Owed
C 01	Touma P/L		
C 02	V Maris		
C 03	Y Yao		
C 04	A Wilson		
C 05	J Dawe		
	TOTALS		

* Hint: Copy the numbers from Scenario 3.3 and only change the accounts affected by the general journal

	Trial Balance to 31/03/20CY		
Accnt No.	Account Name	Debit	Credit
1.10	Cheque Account		
1.113	High Interest Account		
1.12	Accounts Receivable		
1.121	Less Prov'n Doubtful Debts		
1.311	Furniture and Fixtures at Cost		
1.312	Furniture and Fixtures Accum Depn		
2.114	Visa Card		
2.12	Accounts Payable		
2.131	GST Collected		
2.132	GST Paid		
3.11	Owner's Capital		
3.12	Owner Drawings		
4.11	Goldware Sales		
4.12	Jewellery Evaluations		
4.20	Sales Returns		
4.90	Discounts Received		
5.11	Goldware Purchases		
5.12	Purchase of Consumables		
5.20	Purchase Returns		
5.90	Discounts Given		
6.18	Office Supplies		
6.242	Electricity		
8.1	Interest Income		
	TOTALS		

Scenario 3.3 to 3.5 (continued)

Elite Co.

3.5 After contra deal entered

	Schedule of Accounts Receivable as at 31/3/20CY	
Accnt	**Account Name**	**Balance**
C 01	Touma P/L	
C 02	V Maris	
C 03	Y Yao	
C 04	A Wilson	
C 05	J Dawe	
	TOTALS	

	Schedule of Accounts Payable as at 31/3/20CY	
Accnt	**Account Name**	**Balance**
S 01	Bui & Co	
S 02	S Ahuja	
S 03	Cheok & Son	
S 04	Eriser P/L	
S 05	Citipower	
S 06	V Maris	
	TOTALS	

	Trial Balance to 31/03/20CY		
Accnt	**Account Name**	**Debit**	**Credit**
1.10	Cheque Account		
1.113	High Interest Account		
1.12	Accounts Receivable		
1.121	Less Prov'n Doubtful Debts		
1.311	Furniture and Fixtures at Cost		
1.312	Furniture and Fixtures Accum Depn		
2.114	Visa Card		
2.12	Accounts Payable		
2.131	GST Collected		
2.132	GST Paid		
3.11	Owner's Capital		
3.12	Owner Drawings		
4.11	Goldware Sales		
4.12	Jewellery Evaluations		
4.20	Sales Returns		
4.90	Discounts Received		
5.11	Goldware Purchases		
5.12	Purchase of Consumables		
5.20	Purchase Returns		
5.90	Discounts Given		
6.17	Maintenance		
6.18	Office Supplies		
6.242	Electricity		
8.1	Interest Income		
	TOTALS		

Elite Co. General Ledgers

Cheque Account   1.10

Date	Particulars	Folio	Debit	Credit	Balance	
1/3	Opening Balance	GJ1	37,148.00		37,148.00	Dr
1/3	High Interest Bank	GJ1		5,000.00	32,148.00	
2/3	Visa Card	GJ1		300.00	31,848.00	
2/3	Owner Drawings	GJ1		500.00	31,348.00	

High Interest Bank Account   1.113

Date	Particulars	Folio	Debit	Credit	Balance	
1/3	Opening Balance	GJ1	5,000.00		5,000.00	Dr

Accounts Receivable   1.12

Date	Particulars	Folio	Debit	Credit	Balance	
1/3	Opening Balance	SJ1	576.40		576.40	Dr

Less Prov'n for Doubtful Debts   1.121

Date	Particulars	Folio	Debit	Credit	Balance	
1/3	Opening Balance	GJ1		800.00	800.00	Cr

Furniture and Fixtures at cost   1.311

Date	Particulars	Folio	Debit	Credit	Balance	
1/3	Opening Balance	GJ1	9,550.00		9,550.00	Dr

Furniture and Fixtures accum depn   1.312

Date	Particulars	Folio	Debit	Credit	Balance	
1/3	Opening Balance	GJ1		5,604.71	5,604.71	Cr

Visa Card   2.114

Date	Particulars	Folio	Debit	Credit	Balance	
1/3	Opening Balance			1,000.00	1,000.00	Cr
1/3	Cheque Account	GJ1	300.00		700.00	

Elite Co. General Ledgers (continued)

Accounts Payable 2.12

Date	Particulars	Folio	Debit	Credit	Balance	
1/3	Opening Balance			5,148.00	5,148.00	Cr
2/3	Electricity	GJ1		583.00	5,731.00	Cr

GST Collected 2.131

Date	Particulars	Folio	Debit	Credit	Balance	
1/3	Opening Balance			52.40	52.40	Cr

GST Paid 2.132

Date	Particulars	Folio	Debit	Credit	Balance	
1/3	Opening Balance		468.00		468.00	Dr
2/3	Electricity	GJ1	53.00		521.00	Dr

Owner's Capital 3.11

Date	Particulars	Folio	Debit	Credit	Balance	
1/3	Opening Balance	GJ1		35,137.29	35,137.29	Cr

Owners Drawings 3.12

Date	Particulars	Folio	Debit	Credit	Balance	
1/3	Cheque Account	GJ1	500.00		500.00	Dr

Goldware Sales 4.11

Date	Particulars	Folio	Debit	Credit	Balance

Jewellery Evaluations 4.12

Date	Particulars	Folio	Debit	Credit	Balance

Elite Co. General Ledgers (continued)

Sales Returns and Allowanced 4.2

Date	Particulars	Folio	Debit	Credit	Balance

Discount Received 4.90

Date	Particulars	Folio	Debit	Credit	Balance

Goldware Purchases 5.11

Date	Particulars	Folio	Debit	Credit	Balance

Purchase of Consumables 5.12

Date	Particulars	Folio	Debit	Credit	Balance

Purchase Returns and Allowances 5.20

Date	Particulars	Folio	Debit	Credit	Balance

Discounts Given 5.9

Date	Particulars	Folio	Debit	Credit	Balance

Maintenance 6.17

Date	Particulars	Folio	Debit	Credit	Balance

Office Supplies 6.18

Date	Particulars	Folio	Debit	Credit	Balance

Electricity 6.242

Date	Particulars	Folio	Debit	Credit	Balance
2/3	Accounts Payable	GJ1	530.00		530.00

Interest Income 8.1

Date	Particulars	Folio	Debit	Credit	Balance

Exercise 4.1 and 4.2

Alyssa Pty Ltd

General Journal				GJ1
Date	Particulars	Folio	Debit	Credit

Exercise 4.1 and 4.2 (continued)

Alyssa Pty Ltd

Cheque Account						1.10
Date	Particulars	Folio	Debit	Credit	Balance	
31/12	Balance Brought Forward		14,127.84		14,127.84	Dr
						Dr
						Dr
						Dr

Accounts Receivable						1.12
Date	Particulars	Folio	Debit	Credit	Balance	
31/12	Balance Brought Forward		633.40		633.40	Dr

Provision for Doubtful Debts						1.121
Date	Particulars	Folio	Debit	Credit	Balance	
31/12	Balance Brought Forward			120.00	120.00	Cr

Accrued Revenue						1.18
Date	Particulars	Folio	Debit	Credit	Balance	
						Dr
						Dr

Prepayments						1.19
Date	Particulars	Folio	Debit	Credit	Balance	
31/12	Balance Brought Forward		1,350.00		1,350.00	Dr
						Dr

Office Equipment at Cost						1.211
Date	Particulars	Folio	Debit	Credit	Balance	
31/12	Balance Brought forward		9,250.00		9,250.00	Dr
						Dr

Office Equipment Accum Depn						1.212
Date	Particulars	Folio	Debit	Credit	Balance	
31/12	Balance Brought Forward			4,652.85	4,652.85	Cr
						Cr

Motor Vehicles at Cost						1.221
Date	Particulars	Folio	Debit	Credit	Balance	
31/12	Balance Brought Forward		6,000.00		6,000.00	Dr
						Dr
						Dr
						Dr

Motor Vehicles Accum Depn						1.222
Date	Particulars	Folio	Debit	Credit	Balance	
31/12	Balance Brought Forward			3,802.00	3,802.00	Cr
						Cr
						Cr

Exercise 4.1 and 4.2 (continued)

Alyssa Pty Ltd

Accounts Payable | | | | | 2.12

Date	Particulars	Folio	Debit	Credit	Balance	
31/12	Balance Brought Forward	GJ1		722.00	722.00	Cr

GST Collected | | | | | 2.131

Date	Particulars	Folio	Debit	Credit	Balance	
31/12	Opening Balance			37.50	37.50	Cr
						Cr
						Cr

GST Paid | | | | | 2.132

Date	Particulars	Folio	Debit	Credit	Balance	
31/12	Balance Brought Forward	GJ1	245.67		245.67	Dr
						Dr
						Dr
						Dr

Unearned Revenue | | | | | 2.18

Date	Particulars	Folio	Debit	Credit	Balance	
						Cr
						Cr

Accrued Expenses | | | | | 2.19

Date	Particulars	Folio	Debit	Credit	Balance	
						Cr
						Cr

Bank Loan | | | | | 2.20

Date	Particulars	Folio	Debit	Credit	Balance	
						Cr
						Cr

Owner's Capital | | | | | 3.11

Date	Particulars	Folio	Debit	Credit	Balance	
31/12	Balance Brought Forward	GJ1		3,703.56	3,703.56	Cr
						Cr

Sales | | | | | 4.1

Date	Particulars	Folio	Debit	Credit	Balance	
31/12	Balance Brought Forward	GJ1		31,301.00	31,301.00	Cr
						Cr

Sales Returns | | | | | 4.20

Date	Particulars	Folio	Debit	Credit	Balance	
31/12	Balance Brought Forward	GJ1	100.00		100.00	Dr

Purchases | | | | | 5.10

Date	Particulars	Folio	Debit	Credit	Balance	
31/12	Balance Brought Forward	GJ1	12,110.00		12,110.00	Dr

Exercise 4.1 and 4.2 (continued)

Alyssa Pty Ltd

Purchase Returns						5.2	
Date	Particulars	Folio	Debit	Credit	Balance		
31/1	Balance Brought Forward	GJ1		150.00	150.00	Cr

Advertising						6.10	
Date	Particulars	Folio	Debit	Credit	Balance		
						Dr
						Dr

Depreciation						6.11	
Date	Particulars	Folio	Debit	Credit	Balance		
						Dr
						Dr

Insurance						6.14	
Date	Particulars	Folio	Debit	Credit	Balance		
						Dr
						Dr

Office Supplies						6.18	
Date	Particulars	Folio	Debit	Credit	Balance		
31/1	Balance Brought Forward	GJ1	142.00		142.00	Dr

Electricity						6.242	
Date	Particulars	Folio	Debit	Credit	Balance		
31/1	Balance Brought Forward	GJ1	530.00		530.00	Dr

Profit on sale of asset						8.3	
Date	Particulars	Folio	Debit	Credit	Balance		
						Cr

Exercise 4.1 and 4.2 (continued)

Alyssa Pty Ltd

ORIGINAL TRIAL BALANCE (For reference only)

Accnt No.	Account Name	Debit	Credit
	Trial Balance to 31/12/20CY		
1.10	Cheque Account	14,127.84	
1.12	Accounts Receivable	633.40	
1.121	Less Prov'n Doubtful Debts		120.00
1.19	Prepayments	1,350.00	
1.211	Office Equip at Cost	9,250.00	
1.212	Office Equip Accum Depn		4,652.85
1.221	Motor Vehicle at Cost	6,000.00	
1.222	Motor Vehicle Accum Depn		3,802.00
2.12	Accounts Payable		722.00
2.131	GST Collected		37.50
2.132	GST Paid	245.67	
2.20	Bank Loan		
3.11	Owner's Capital		3,703.56
4.1	Sales		31,301.00
4.2	Sales Returns	100.00	
5.1	Purchases	12,110.00	
5.2	Purchaes Returns		150.00
6.18	Office Supplies	142.00	
6.242	Electricity	530.00	
	TOTALS	44,488.91	44,488.91

AFTER 4.1: Copy from the trial balance above and only update the accounts affected by the general journals

Accnt No.	Account Name	Debit	Credit
	Trial Balance to 31/01/20CY		
1.10	Cheque Account		
1.12	Accounts Receivable		
1.121	Less Prov'n Doubtful Debts		
1.19	Prepayments		
1.211	Office Equip at Cost		
1.212	Office Equip Accum Depn		
1.221	Motor Vehicle at Cost		
1.222	Motor Vehicle Accum Depn		
2.12	Accounts Payable		
2.131	GST Collected		
2.132	GST Paid		
2.20	Bank Loan		
3.11	Owner's Capital		
4.1	Sales		
4.2	Sales Returns		
5.1	Purchases		
5.2	Purchase Returns		
6.18	Office Supplies		
6.242	Electricity		
	TOTALS		

Exercise 4.1 and 4.2 (continued)

Alyssa Pty Ltd

Asset Code	Description	Acquisition Date	Cost (Excl GST)	Disposal Date	Sale Price (Excl GST)
Alyssa Pty Ltd					
Asset Register					
As at 31/01/CY					
1.211	**Office Equipment**				
1.211.1	Printer/Copier (Samsung XLT-1000)	10/9/14	$2,300.00		
1.211.2	Mac Airbook (S.N 015C-DM-35684)	23/12/14	$3,500.00		
1.211.3	Server (S.N 123-C567-2243892)	2/1/15	$3,450.00		
		TOTAL			
1.221	**Motor Vehicles**				
1.221.1	Transit Van (rego 1FM-261)	1/7/14	$6,000.00		
		TOTAL			

AFTER Exercise 4.2

Accnt No.	Account Name	Debit	Credit
Trial Balance			
to 31/01/20CY			
1.10	Cheque Account		
1.12	Accounts Receivable		
1.121	Less Prov'n Doubtful Debts		
1.18	Accrued Revenue		
1.19	Prepayments		
1.211	Office Equip at Cost		
1.212	Office Equip Accum Depn		
1.221	Motor Vehicle at Cost		
1.222	Motor Vehicle Accum Depn		
2.12	Accounts Payable		
2.131	GST Collected		
2.132	GST Paid		
2.18	Unearned Revenue		
2.19	Accrued Expenses		
2.20	Bank Loan		
3.11	Owner's Capital		
4.1	Sales		
4.2	Sales Returns		
5.1	Purchases		
5.2	Purchase Returns		
6.10	Advertising		
6.11	Depreciation		
6.14	Insurance		
6.18	Office Supplies		
6.242	Electricity		
8.3	Profit on Sale of Asset		
	TOTALS		

Scenario 4.1 and 4.2

Elite Co

Scenario 4.1 Trial Balance before scenarios

Accnt No.	Account Name	Debit	Credit
	Trial Balance to 31/03/20CY		
1.10	Cheque Account	30,868.50	
1.113	High Interest Account	5,000.00	
1.12	Accounts Receivable	6,215.00	
1.121	Less Prov'n Doubtful Debts		426.00
1.311	Furniture and Fixtures at Cost	9,550.00	
1.312	Furniture and Fixtures Accum Depn		5,604.71
2.114	Visa Card		700.00
2.12	Accounts Payable		18,909.00
2.131	GST Collected		1,973.70
2.132	GST Paid	3,174.20	
3.11	Owner's Capital		35,137.29
3.12	Owner's Drawings	500.00	
4.11	Goldware Sales		11,722.00
4.12	Jewellery Evaluations		8,500.00
4.20	Sales Returns	600.00	
4.90	Discounts Received		170.00
5.11	Goldware Purchases	21,960.00	
5.12	Purchase of Consumables	5,000.00	
5.20	Purchase Returns		2,000.00
5.90	Discounts Given	35.00	
6.17	Maintenance	1,600.00	
6.18	Office Supplies	142.00	
6.242	Electricity	530.00	
8.1	Interest Income		32.00
	TOTALS	85,174.70	85,174.70

Scenario 4.1 and 4.2 (continued)

Elite Co

Elite Co Asset Register As at 31/03/CY					
Asset Code	Description	Acquisition Date	Cost (Excl GST)	Disposal Date	Sale Price (Excl GST)
1.311	**Furniture and Fixtures**				
1.311.1	Original Shop Fitout	1/7/11	$8,050.00		
1.311.2	Jewellers Desk	23/12/12	$1,500.00		
		TOTAL			
1.321	**Input New Asset Category Here**				
		TOTAL			

Scenario 4.1 and 4.2 (continued)

Elite Co

The accounts general ledger can be found starting at page 57

General Journal				GJ2
Date	Particulars	Folio	Debit	Credit

Scenario 4.1 and 4.2 (continued)

Elite Co

Scenario 4.2 Trial Balance after journals
(remember to update from your general ledger workbook)

Accnt No.	Account Name	Debit	Credit
Trial Balance to 31/03/20CY			
1.10	Cheque Account		
1.113	High Interest Account		
1.12	Accounts Receivable		
1.121	Less Prov'n Doubtful Debts		
1.13	Inventory		
1.18	Accrued Revenue		
1.22	Prepayments		
1.311	Furniture and Fixtures at Cost		
1.312	Furniture and Fixtures Accum Depn		
2.114	Visa Card		
2.12	Accounts Payable		
2.131	GST Collected		
2.132	GST Paid		
2.16	Unearned Revenue		
2.19	Accrued Expenses		
2.20	Bank Loan		
3.11	Owner's Capital		
3.12	Owner's Drawings		
4.11	Goldware Sales		
4.12	Jewellery Evaluations		
4.20	Sales Returns		
4.90	Discounts Received		
5.11	Goldware Purchases		
5.12	Purchase of Consumables		
5.20	Purchase Returns		
5.90	Discounts Given		
6.10	Advertising		
6.11	Depreciation		
6.12	Bad Debt		
6.17	Maintenance		
6.18	Office Supplies		
6.242	Electricity		
7.1	Cost of Goods Sold		
8.1	Interest Income		
8.3	Profit on Sale of Asset		
	TOTALS		

Exercise 4.3

Alyssa Pty Ltd

Date	Particulars		Folio	Debit	Credit
	General Journal				GJ2

Exercise 4.3 (continued)

Alyssa Pty Ltd

Cheque Account   1.10

Date	Particulars	Folio	Debit	Credit	Balance	
31/12	Balance Brought Forward		14,127.84		14,127.84	Dr
15/1	Office Equip at Cost	GJ1		1,320.00	12,807.84	Dr
31/1	Motor Vehicle at Cost	GJ1	2,750.00		15,557.84	Dr
31/1	Unearned Revenue	GJ1	550.00		16,107.84	Dr

Accounts Receivable   1.12

Date	Particulars	Folio	Debit	Credit	Balance	
1/3	Balance Brought Forward	SJ1	30.40		30.40	Dr
31/1	Sales Journal	SJ1	916.00		946.40	Dr
31/1	Sales Returns	SR1		100.00	846.40	Dr
31/1	Cash Receipts	CR1		213.00	633.40	Dr

Less Prov'n for Doubtful Debts   1.121

Date	Particulars	Folio	Debit	Credit	Balance	
31/1	Opening Balance	GJ1		120.00	120.00	Cr

Accrued Revenue   1.18

Date	Particulars	Folio	Debit	Credit	Balance	
31/1	Sales	GJ1	3,300.00		3,300.00	Dr

Prepayments   1.19

Date	Particulars	Folio	Debit	Credit	Balance	
31/12	Balance Brought Forward		1,350.00		1,350.00	Dr
31/1	Insurance	GJ1		150.00	1,200.00	Dr

Office Equipment at Cost   1.211

Date	Particulars	Folio	Debit	Credit	Balance	
31/12	Balance Brought Forward		9,250.00		9,250.00	Dr
15/1	Cheque Account	GJ1	1,200.00		10,450.00	Dr

Office Equipment Accum Depn   1.212

Date	Particulars	Folio	Debit	Credit	Balance	
31/12	Balance Brought Forward			4,652.85	4,652.85	Cr
31/1	Depreciation	GJ1		64.97	4,717.82	Cr

Motor Vehicles at Cost   1.221

Date	Particulars	Folio	Debit	Credit	Balance	
31/12	Balance Brought Forward	GJ1	6,000.00		6,000.00	Dr
1/1	Bank Loan	GJ1	17,500.00		23,500.00	Dr
31/1	Cheque Account	GJ1		2,500.00	21,000.00	Dr
31/1	Motor Vehicle Accum Depn	GJ1		3,500.00	17,500.00	Dr

Motor Vehicles Accum Depn   1.222

Date	Particulars	Folio	Debit	Credit	Balance	
31/12	Balance Brought Forward			3,802.00	3,802.00	Cr
31/1	Depreciation	GJ1		391.67	4,193.67	Cr
31/1	Motor Vehicle at Cost	GJ1	4,193.67		0.00	Cr

Exercise 4.3 (continued)

Alyssa Pty Ltd

Accounts Payable   2.12

Date	Particulars	Folio	Debit	Credit	Balance	
31/1	Balance Brought forward			130.00	130.00	Cr
31/1		PJ1		683.00	813.00	Cr
31/1		CP1	91.00		722.00	Cr

GST Collected   2.131

Date	Particulars	Folio	Debit	Credit	Balance	
31/1	Opening Balance			37.50	37.50	Cr
31/1	Motor Vehicle at Cost	GJ1		250.00	287.50	Cr
31/1	Unearned Revenue	GJ1		50.00	337.50	Cr

GST Paid   2.132

Date	Particulars	Folio	Debit	Credit	Balance	
31/12	Balance Brought Forward	GJ1	245.67		245.67	Dr
15/1	Office Equip at Cost	GJ1	120.00		365.67	Dr
31/1	Motor Vehicles at Cost	GJ1	1,750.00		2,115.67	Dr

Unearned Revenue   2.18

Date	Particulars	Folio	Debit	Credit	Balance	
31/1	Cheque Account	GJ1		550.00	550.00	Cr

Accrued Expenses   2.19

Date	Particulars	Folio	Debit	Credit	Balance	
31/1	Advertising	GJ1		120.00	120.00	Cr

Bank Loan   2.20

Date	Particulars	Folio	Debit	Credit	Balance	
31/1	Motor Vehicles at Cost	GJ1		19,250.00	19,250.00	Cr

Owner Capital   3.11

Date	Particulars	Folio	Debit	Credit	Balance	
31/12	Balance Brought Forward	GJ1		3,703.56	3,703.56	Cr

Current Earnings   3.9

Date	Particulars	Folio	Debit	Credit	Balance	
						Cr

Sales   4.1

Date	Particulars	Folio	Debit	Credit	Balance	
31/12	Balance Brought Forward	GJ1		31,301.00	31,301.00	Cr
31/1	Accrued Revenue	GJ1		3,000.00	34,301.00	Cr

Exercise 4.3 (continued)

Alyssa Pty Ltd

Sales Returns						4.2	
Date	Particulars	Folio	Debit	Credit	Balance		
31/1	Sales Returns	SR1	100.00		100.00	Dr
						Dr

Purchases						5.1	
Date	Particulars	Folio	Debit	Credit	Balance		
31/1	Purchases Journal	PJ1	12,110.00		12,110.00	Dr
						Dr
						Dr

Purchase Returns						5.2	
Date	Particulars	Folio	Debit	Credit	Balance		
31/1	Purchase Returns	PG1		150.00	150.00	Cr

Advertising						6.10	
Date	Particulars	Folio	Debit	Credit	Balance		
31/1	Accrued Expenses	GJ1	120.00		120.00	Dr

Depreciation						6.11	
Date	Particulars	Folio	Debit	Credit	Balance		
31/1	Motor Vehicle Accum Depn	GJ1	456.64		456.64	Dr

Insurance						6.14	
Date	Particulars	Folio	Debit	Credit	Balance		
31/1	Prepayments	GJ1	150.00		150.00	Dr

Office Supplies						6.18	
Date	Particulars	Folio	Debit	Credit	Balance		
31/1	Cash Payments	CP1	142.00		142.00	Dr

Electricity						6.242	
Date	Particulars	Folio	Debit	Credit	Balance		
31/1	Accounts Payable	GJ1	530.00		530.00	Dr

Exercise 4.3 (continued)

Alyssa Pty Ltd

Cost of Goods Sold						7.1
Date	Particulars	Folio	Debit	Credit	Balance	

Trading Account						7.2
Date	Particulars	Folio	Debit	Credit	Balance	

Profit and Loss						7.3
Date	Particulars	Folio	Debit	Credit	Balance	

Profit on Sale of Asset						8.3
Date	Particulars	Folio	Debit	Credit	Balance	
31/1	Motor vehicle Accum depn	GJ1		693.67	693.67	Cr

AFTER 4.3

	Trial Balance to 31/01/20CY		
Accnt No.	Account Name	Debit	Credit
1.10	Cheque Account		
1.12	Accounts Receivable		
1.121	Less Prov'n Doubtful Debts		
1.18	Accrued Revenue		
1.19	Prepayments		
1.211	Office Equip at Cost		
1.212	Office Equip Accum Depn		
1.221	Motor Vehicle at Cost		
1.222	Motor Vehicle Accum Depn		
2.12	Accounts Payable		
2.131	GST Collected		
2.132	GST Paid		
2.18	Unearned Revenue		
2.19	Accrued Expenses		
2.2	Bank Loan		
3.11	Owner's Capital		
3.9	Current Earnings		
	TOTALS		

Scenario 4.3

Elite Co

The accounts general ledgers start on page 57

	General Journal			GJ3
Date	Particulars	Folio	Debit	Credit

Scenario 4.3 (continued)

Elite Co

Scenario 4.3 After closing general journals

Accnt No.	Account Name	Debit	Credit
	Trial Balance **to 31/03/20CY**		
1.10	Cheque Account		
1.113	High Interest Account		
1.12	Accounts Receivable		
1.121	Less Prov'n Doubtful Debts		
1.13	Inventory		
1.18	Accrued Revenue		
1.22	Prepayments		
1.311	Furniture and Fixtures at Cost		
1.312	Furniture and Fixtures Accum Depn		
2.114	Visa Card		
2.12	Accounts Payable		
2.131	GST Collected		
2.132	GST Paid		
2.16	Unearned Revenue		
2.19	Accrued Expenses		
2.20	Bank Loan		
3.11	Owner's Capital		
3.12	Owner's Drawings		
3.9	Current Earnings		
4.11	Goldware Sales		
4.12	Jewellery Evaluations		
4.20	Sales Returns		
4.90	Discounts Received		
5.11	Goldware Purchases		
5.12	Purchase of Consumables		
5.20	Purchase Returns		
5.90	Discounts Given		
6.10	Advertising		
6.11	Depreciation		
6.12	Bad Debt		
6.17	Maintenance		
6.18	Office Supplies		
6.242	Electricity		
8.1	Interest Income		
8.3	Profit on sale of Asset		
	TOTALS		

Exercise 4.4

Alyssa Pty Ltd

REVENUE STATEMENT for Alyssa Pty Ltd FOR JANUARY 2016			
Account Name			
INCOME			
Net Sales			
TOTAL SALES			
Less Cost of Goods Sold			
TOTAL COST OF GOODS SOLD			
TOTAL GROSS PROFIT			
OPERATING EXPENSES			
Advertising			
Depreciation Expense			
Insurance			
Office Supplies			
Electricity			
TOTAL OPERATING EXPENSES			
OPERATING PROFIT			
Add Other Income			
Less Other Expenses			
TOTAL PROFIT			

Exercise 4.4 (continued)

Alyssa Pty Ltd

Account Name			
BALANCE SHEET			
for Alyssa Pty Ltd			
FOR JANUARY 2016			
ASSET			
CURRENT ASSETS			
Cheque Account			
Accounts Receivable			
Prov'n for Doubtful Debts			
Accrued revenue			
Prepayments			
TOTAL CURRENT ASSETS			
FIXED ASSETS			
Office Equipment at Cost			
Office Equipment Accum Depn			
Motor Vehicle at Cost			
Motor Vehicle Accum Depn			
TOTAL FIXED ASSETS			
TOTAL ASSETS			
LIABILITIES			
CURRENT LIABILITIES			
Accounts Payable			
GST LIABILITIES			
GST Collected			
GST Paid			
TOTAL GST LIABILITIES			
Unearned Revenue			
Accrued Expenses			
TOTAL CURRENT LIABILITIES			
NON-CURRENT LIABILITIES			
Bank Loan			
TOTAL NON CURRENT LIABILITIES			
TOTAL LIABILITIES			
NET ASSETS			
EQUITY			
OWNER'S EQUITY			
Owner's Capital			
Owner's Drawings			
TOTAL OWNER'S EQUITY			
Current Year Earnings			
TOTAL EQUITY			

Scenario 4.4

Elite Co

Account Name			
REVENUE STATEMENT for Elite Co FOR MARCH 2016			
INCOME			
Net Sales			
TOTAL SALES			
Less Cost of Goods Sold			
Opening stock			
Net Purchases			
Less Closing Stock			
TOTAL COST OF GOODS SOLD			
TOTAL GROSS PROFIT			
OPERATING EXPENSES			
Advertising			
Depreciation Expense			
Bad Debt Expense			
Maintenance			
Office Supplies			
Electricity			
TOTAL OPERATING EXPENSES			
OPERATING PROFIT			
Add Other Income			
Less Other Expenses			
TOTAL PROFIT			

Scenario 4.4 (continued)
Elite Co

Account Name			
BALANCE SHEET **for Elite Co** **FOR MARCH 2016**			
Account Name			
ASSET			
CURRENT ASSETS			
Cheque Account			
High Interest Bank			
Accounts Receivable			
Prov'n for Doubtful Debts			
Inventory			
Accrued Revenue			
Prepayments			
TOTAL CURRENT ASSETS			
FIXED ASSETS			
Furniture and Fixtures at Cost			
Furniture and Fixtures Accum Depn			
TOTAL FIXED ASSETS			
TOTAL ASSETS			
LIABILITIES			
CURRENT LIABILITIES			
Visa Card			
Accounts Payable			
GST LIABILITIES			
GST Collected			
GST Paid			
TOTAL GST LIABILITIES			
Unearned Revenue			
Accrued Expenses			
TOTAL CURRENT LIABILITIES			
NON-CURRENT LIABILITIES			
Bank Loan			
TOTAL NON CURRENT LIABILITIES			
TOTAL LIABILITIES			
NET ASSETS			
EQUITY			
OWNER'S EQUITY			
Owner's Capital			
Owner's Drawings			
TOTAL OWNER'S EQUITY			
Current Year Earnings			
TOTAL EQUITY			

Elite Co. General Ledgers

Cheque Account — 1.10

Date	Particulars	Folio	Debit	Credit	Balance	
1/3	Opening Balance	GJ1	37,148.00		37,148.00	Dr
1/3	High Interest Bank	GJ1		5,000.00	32,148.00	Dr
2/3	Visa Card	GJ1		300.00	31,848.00	Dr
2/3	Owner's Drawings	GJ1		500.00	31,348.00	Dr
31/3	Cash Payments	CP1		14,357.20	16,990.80	Dr
31/3	Cash Receipts	CR1	13,877.70		30,868.50	Dr

High Interest Bank Account — 1.113

Date	Particulars	Folio	Debit	Credit	Balance	
1/3	Opening Balance	GJ1	5,000.00		5,000.00	Dr

Accounts Receivable — 1.12

Date	Particulars	Folio	Debit	Credit	Balance	
1/3	Opening Balance	SJ1	576.40		576.40	Dr
31/3	Sales Journal	SJ1	11,660.00		12,236.40	Dr
31/3	Sales Returns	SR1		660.00	11,576.40	Dr
31/3	Cash receipts	CR1		35.00	11,541.40	Dr
31/3	Cash receipts	CR1		3.50	11,537.90	Dr
31/3	Cash receipts	CR1		4,911.50	6,626.40	Dr
31/3	Less Prov'n Doubt Debt	GJ1		411.40	6,215.00	Dr
31/3	Jewellery Evaluation	GJ1	1,650.00		7,865.00	Dr
31/3	Accounts Payable	GJ1		1,650.00	6,215.00	Dr

Less Prov'n for Doubtful Debts — 1.121

Date	Particulars	Folio	Debit	Credit	Balance	
1/3	Opening Balance	GJ1		800.00	800.00	Cr
31/3	Accounts Receivable	GJ1	374.00		426.00	Cr

Inventory — 1.13

Date	Particulars	Folio	Debit	Credit	Balance	
						Dr

Accrued revenue — 1.18

Date	Particulars	Folio	Debit	Credit	Balance	
						Dr

Prepayments — 1.22

Date	Particulars	Folio	Debit	Credit	Balance	
						Dr

Furniture and Fixtures at cost — 1.311

Date	Particulars	Folio	Debit	Credit	Balance	
1/3	Opening Balance	GJ1	9,550.00		9,550.00	Dr

Elite Co. General Ledgers (continued)

Furniture and Fixtures accum depn					1.312	
Date	Particulars	Folio	Debit	Credit	Balance	
1/3	Opening Balance	GJ1		5,604.71	5,604.71	Cr

Visa Card					2.114	
Date	Particulars	Folio	Debit	Credit	Balance	
28/2	Balance brought forward	GJ1		1,000.00	1,000.00	Cr
1/3	Cheque Account	GJ1	300.00		700.00	Cr

Accounts Payable					2.12	
Date	Particulars	Folio	Debit	Credit	Balance	
28/2	Balance Brought forward			5,148.00	5,148.00	Cr
2/3	Electricity	GJ1		583.00	5,731.00	Cr
31/3	Purchases Journal	PJ1		24,156.00	29,887.00	Cr
31/3	Purchase Returns	PR1	2,200.00		27,687.00	Cr
31/3	Cash Payments	CP1	170.00		27,517.00	Cr
31/3	Cash Payments	CP1	17.00		27,500.00	Cr
31/3	Cash Payments	CP1	8,701.00		18,799.00	Cr
31/3	Maintenance	GJ1		1,760.00	20,559.00	Cr
31/3	Accounts Receivable	GJ1	1,650.00		18,909.00	Cr

GST Collected					2.131	
Date	Particulars	Folio	Debit	Credit	Balance	
1/3	Opening Balance			52.40	52.40	Cr
31/3	Sales Journal	SJ1		1,060.00	1,112.40	Cr
31/3	Sales Returns	SR1	60.00		1,052.40	Cr
31/3	Cash Receipts	CR1	3.50		1,048.90	Cr
31/3	Cash Receipts	CR1		812.20	1,861.10	Cr
31/3	Less Prov'n Doubtful Debt	GJ1	37.40		1,823.70	Cr
31/3	Accounts Receivable	GJ1		150.00	1,973.70	Cr

GST Paid					2.132	
Date	Particulars	Folio	Debit	Credit	Balance	
28/2	Balance Brought forward		468.00		468.00	Dr
2/3	Electricity	GJ1	53.00		521.00	Dr
31/3	Purchase Journal	PJ1	2,196.00		2,717.00	Dr
31/3	Purchase Returns	PR1		200.00	2,517.00	Dr
31/3	Cash Payments	CP1		17.00	2,500.00	Dr
31/3	Cash Payments	CP1	514.20		3,014.20	Dr
31/3	Accounts payable	GJ1	160.00		3,174.20	Dr

Unearned Revenue					2.16	
Date	Particulars	Folio	Debit	Credit	Balance	
						Cr

Elite Co. General Ledgers (continued)

Accrued expenses					2.19	
Date	Particulars	Folio	Debit	Credit	Balance	
						Cr

Bank Loan					2.20	
Date	Particulars	Folio	Debit	Credit	Balance	
						Cr

Owner's Capital					3.11	
Date	Particulars	Folio	Debit	Credit	Balance	
1/3	Opening Balance	GJ1		35,137.29	35,137.29	Cr

Owner's Drawings					3.12	
Date	Particulars	Folio	Debit	Credit	Balance	
1/3	Cheque Account	GJ1	500.00		500.00	Dr

Current Earnings					3.9	
Date	Particulars	Folio	Debit	Credit	Balance	
						Cr

Goldware Sales					4.11	
Date	Particulars	Folio	Debit	Credit	Balance	
31/3	Sales Journal	SJ1		10,600.00	10,600.00	Cr
31/3	Cash Receipts	CR1		1,122.00	11,722.00	Cr

Jewellery Evalutions					4.12	
Date	Particulars	Folio	Debit	Credit	Balance	
31/3	Cash Payments	CP1		7,000.00	7,000.00	Cr
31/3	Accounts Payable	GJ1		1,500.00	8,500.00	Cr

Sales Returns and Allowances					4.20	
Date	Particulars	Folio	Debit	Credit	Balance	
31/3	Sales Journal	SJ1	600.00		600.00	Dr

Discount Received					4.90	
Date	Particulars	Folio	Debit	Credit	Balance	
31/3	Cash Payments	CP1		170.00	170.00	Cr

Goldware Purchases					5.11	
Date	Particulars	Folio	Debit	Credit	Balance	
31/3	Purchases Journal	PJ1	21,960.00		21,960.00	Dr

Purchase of Consumables					5.12	
Date	Particulars	Folio	Debit	Credit	Balance	
31/3	Cash Payments	CP1	5,000.00		5,000.00	Dr

Elite Co. General Ledgers (continued)

Purchase Returns and Allowances					5.20	
Date	Particulars	Folio	Debit	Credit	Balance	
31/3	Purchase Returns	CR1		2,000.00	2,000.00	Cr

Discounts Given					5.90	
Date	Particulars	Folio	Debit	Credit	Balance	
31/3	Cash Payments	CP1	35.00		35.00	Dr

Advertising					6.10	
Date	Particulars	Folio	Debit	Credit	Balance	

Depreciation					6.11	
Date	Particulars	Folio	Debit	Credit	Balance	
						Dr
						Dr

Bad Debt					6.12	
Date	Particulars	Folio	Debit	Credit	Balance	
						Dr
						Dr

Maintenance					6.17	
Date	Particulars	Folio	Debit	Credit	Balance	
31/3	Accounts Payable	GJ1	1,600.00		1,600.00	Dr
						Dr

Office Supplies					6.18	
Date	Particulars	Folio	Debit	Credit	Balance	
31/3	Cash Payments	CP1	142.00		142.00	Dr

Electricity					6.242	
Date	Particulars	Folio	Debit	Credit	Balance	
2/3	Accounts Payable	GJ1	530.00		530.00	Dr

Cost of Goods Sold					7.1	
Date	Particulars	Folio	Debit	Credit	Balance	
						Cr
						Dr

Trading Account					7.2	
Date	Particulars	Folio	Debit	Credit	Balance	
						Cr
						Cr

Elite Co. General Ledgers (continued)

Profit and Loss					7.3	
Date	Particulars	Folio	Debit	Credit	Balance	
						Cr
						Cr
						Cr

Interest Income					8.1	
Date	Particulars	Folio	Debit	Credit	Balance	
31/3	Cash Receipts	CR1		32.00	32.00	Cr

Profit on sale of Asset					8.3	
Date	Particulars	Folio	Debit	Credit	Balance	
						Cr
						Cr

Scenario 5.3

Elite Co

	General Journal				GJ2
Date	Particulars	Folio	Debit	Credit	

Rent					6.21	
Date	Particulars	Folio	Debit	Credit	Balance	
2/3	Accounts Payable	GJ1	530.00		530.00	Dr
						Dr

Electricity					6.242	
Date	Particulars	Folio	Debit	Credit	Balance	
						Dr

Scenario 5.4

Elite Co

CHEQUE REQUISITION		
REQUESTER INFORMATION		
Name: _____	**Ext:** _____	
Dept: _____	**Date:** _____	
VENDOR INFORMATION		
Name on Cheque: _____		
Address: _____		
_____		
_____		
PAYMENT DESCRIPTION		
Reason for Cheque	**Account**	**Amount**
	Cheque total:	_____
Signed:	Authorised:	
	Chq No:	

CHEQUE REQUISITION		
REQUESTER INFORMATION		
Name: _____	**Ext:** _____	
Dept: _____	**Date:** _____	
VENDOR INFORMATION		
Name on Cheque: _____		
Address: _____		
_____		
_____		
PAYMENT DESCRIPTION		
Reason for Cheque	**Account**	**Amount**
	Cheque total:	_____
Signed:	Authorised:	
	Chq No:	

Scenario 5.4 (continued)

Elite Co

Cash Payments Journal												
Date	Chq No.	Particulars	Folio	Discnt	GST Adj	Acct Payable	GST Paid	Prchses	GST Paid	General	Bank

Citipower   S 05

Date	Particulars	Debit	Credit	Balance	
2/3	Electricity		583.00	583.00	Cr
					Cr

Global Insurance   S 07

Date	Particulars	Debit	Credit	Balance	
31/3	Prepayments		825.00	825.00	Cr
					Cr

Exercise 6.1

Abel Co.

Abel Co Timesheet							
Name:	Ron Hall			**Pay end:**		28/02/CY	
DATE	**START**	**STOP**	**HOURS**	**NORM**	**1.5X**	**2X**	**3X**
15/2	8:00	12:00	4:00				
	12:30	15:30	3:00				
16/2	8:00	12:00	4:00				
	12:30	15:30	3:00				
17/2	8:00	12:00	4:00				
	12:30	15:30	3:00				
18/2	8:00	12:00	4:00				
	12:30	15:30	3:00				
19/2	8:00	12:00	4:00				
	12:30	16:00	3:30				
20/2	8:00	12:00	4:00				
21/2							
22/2	8:00	12:00	4:00				
	12:30	15:30	3:00				
23/2	8:00	12:00	4:00				
	12:30	15:30	3:00				
24/2	8:00	12:00	4:00				
	12:30	15:30	3:00				
25/2	8:00	12:00	4:00				
	12:30	15:30	3:00				
26/2	8:00	12:00	4:00				
	12:30	16:00	3:30				
27/2							
28/2							
			TOTALS				

Signed :   Ron Hall   Date: 27/02/20CY
Authorised: MF   Date: 29/02/20CY

Abel Co. Wages Calculation Card		F/night End: 28/02/CY		
Name: Ron Hall		**Base hourly rate:**		$20.00
	Actual Hours	**Adjusted Hours**		**Amount**
Normal time			$	
Time and a half		(x1.5)	$	
Double Time		(x2)	$	
Triple time		(x3)	$	
Personal Leave			$	
Annual Leave			$	
Leave Loading 17.5%			$	
Less Salary Sacrifice			$	
GROSS PAY			$	
DEDUCTIONS				
PAYG TAX	$			
LESS Rebate	$			
NET Tax deducted		$		
Additional Super		$		
Savings Plan		$		
Trade Union		$		
Health Insurance		$		
TOTAL DEDUCTIONS			$	
NET PAY			$	

Pay Slip	
Abel Co. ABN 22 331 231 322	
Name:	Ron Hall
Pay Ending:	28/02/CY
Normal Wage	
Overtime	
Personal/Holiday	
Less Sal Sacrifice	
GROSS PAY	
Deductions	
Tax	
Additional Super	
Savings	
Union	
Health	
Total Deductions	
Net Pay	
Super Fund	Spectrum Super
Super Amount	

Exercise 6.1 (continued)

Abel Co.

Abel Co Timesheet							
Name:	Liz Toll			Pay end:		28/02/CY	
DATE	**START**	**STOP**	**HOURS**	**NORM**	**1.5X**	**2X**	**3X**
15/2	8:00	12:00	4:00				
	12:30	16:00	3:30				
16/2	8:00	12:00	4:00				
	12:30	16:00	3:30				
17/2	8:00	12:00	4:00				
	12:30	16:00	3:30				
18/2	8:00	12:00	4:00				
	12:30	16:00	3:30				
19/2	8:00	12:00	4:00				
	12:30	16:00	3:30				
20/2							
21/2							
22/2	8:00	12:00	4:00				
	12:30	16:00	3:30				
23/2	8:00	12:00	4:00				
	12:30	16:00	3:30				
24/2	8:00	12:00	4:00				
	12:30	16:00	3:30				
25/2	8:00	12:00	4:00				
	12:30	16:00	3:30				
26/2	8:00	12:00	4:00				
	12:30	16:00	3:30				
27/2							
28/2							
			TOTALS				
Signed :	Liz Toll			Date: 27/02/20CY			
Authorised:	MF			Date: 29/02/20CY			

Abel Co. Wages Calculation Card		F/night End: 28/02/CY		
Name: Liz Toll		Base hourly rate:		$15.00
	Actual Hours	**Adjusted Hours**	**Amount**	
Normal time			$	
Time and a half		(x1.5)	$	
Double Time		(x2)	$	
Triple time		(x3)	$	
Personal Leave			$	
Annual Leave			$	
Leave Loading 17.5%			$	
Less Salary Sacrifice			$	
GROSS PAY			$	
DEDUCTIONS				
PAYG TAX	$			
LESS Rebate	$			
NET Tax deducted		$		
Additional Super		$		
Savings Plan		$		
Trade Union		$		
Health Insurance		$		
TOTAL DEDUCTIONS			$	
NET PAY			$	

Pay Slip	
Abel Co. ABN 22 331 231 322	
Name:	Liz Toll
Pay Ending:	28/02/CY
Normal Wage	
Overtime	
Personal/Holiday	
Less Sal Sacrifice	
GROSS PAY	
Deductions	
Tax	
Additional Super	
Savings	
Union	
Health	
Total Deductions	
Net Pay	
Super Fund	Spectrum Super
Super Amount	

Scenario 6.2

Elite Co.

Elite Co Timesheet							
Name:	Janet Holmes			**Pay end:**		08/03/CY	
DATE	**START**	**STOP**	**HOURS**	**NORM**	**1.5X**	**2X**	**3X**
24/2	9:00	13:00	4:00	4.00			
	13:30	16:30	3:00	3.00			
25/2	8:00	12:00	4:00	4.00			
	13:00	16:00	3:00	3.00			
26/2	8:00	12:00	4:00	4.00			
	12:30	16:00	3:30	3.00			
27/2							
28/2							
29/2	8:00	14:00	6:00	6.00			
	14:45	18:15	3:30	1.00	2.00	0.50	
01/03	8:30	12:00	3:30	3.50			
	12:30	16:00	3:30	3.50			
02/03	8:00	12:00	4:00	4.00			
	13:00	16:00	3:00	3.00			
03/03	8:00	12:00	4:00	4.00			
	13:00	16:00	3:00	3.00			
04/03	8:00	12:00	4:00	4.00			
	13:00	16:00	3:00	3.00			
05/03							
06/03							
07/03	8:00	12:00	4:00	4.00			
	12:30	15:30	3:00	3.00			
28/03	8:00	12:00	4:00	4.00			
	12:30	15:30	3:00	3.00			
		TOTALS		70.00	2.00	0.50	
Signed :	Janet Homes			Date: 8/03/20CY			
Authorised:	MF			Date: 9/03/20CY			

Elite Co. Wages Calculation Card		F/night End: 08/03/CY		
Name: Janet Holmes		**Base hourly rate:**	$18.00	
	Actual Hours	**Adjusted Hours**	**Amount**	
Normal time			$	
Time and a half		(x1.5)	$	
Double Time		(x2)	$	
Triple time		(x3)	$	
Personal Leave			$	
Annual Leave			$	
Leave Loading 17.5%			$	
Less Salary Sacrifice			$	
GROSS PAY			$	
DEDUCTIONS				
PAYG TAX	$			
LESS Rebate	$			
NET Tax deducted		$		
Additional Super		$		
Savings Plan		$		
Trade Union		$		
Health Insurance		$		
TOTAL DEDUCTIONS			$	
NET PAY			$	

Pay Slip	
Elite Co. ABN 11 111 111 111	
Name:	Janet Holmes
Pay Ending:	08/03/CY
Normal Wage	
Overtime	
Personal/Holiday	
Less Sal Sacrifice	
GROSS PAY	
Deductions	
Tax	
Additional Super	
Savings	
Union	
Health	
Total Deductions	
Net Pay	
Super Fund	Spectrum Super
Super Amount	

Scenario 6.2 (continued)

Elite Co.

Elite Co Timesheet							
Name:	Jo Mendez			**Pay end:**		08/03/CY	
DATE	**START**	**STOP**	**HOURS**	**NORM**	**1.5X**	**2X**	**3X**
24/2	9:00	12:00	3:00	4.00			
	12:30	15:30	3:00	3.00			
25/2	8:00	12:00	4:00	4.00			
	12:30	15:30	3:00	3.00			
26/2	8:00	12:00	4:00	4.00			
	12:30	15:30	3:00	3.00			
27/2							
28/2							
29/2	8:00	12:00	4:00	4.00			
	12:30	15:30	3:00	3.00			
01/03	8:00	12:00	4:00	4.00			
	12:30	16:00	3:30	3.00	0.50		
02/03	8:00	12:00	4:00	4.00			
	12:30	15:30	3:00	3.00			
03/03	8:00	12:00	4:00	4.00			
	12:30	15:30	3:00	3.00			
04/03	8:00	12:00	4:00	4.00			
	12:30	15:30	3:00	3.00			
05/03							
06/03							
07/03	8:00	12:00	4:00	4.00			
	12:30	15:30	3:00	3.00			
28/03	8:00	12:00	4:00	4.00			
	12:30	16:00	3:30	3.00	0.50		
		TOTALS		70.00	1.00		
Signed :	Jo Mendez				Date: 8/03/20CY		
Authorised:	MF				Date: 9/03/20CY		

Elite Co. Wages Calculation Card		F/night End: 08/03/CY		
Name: Jo Mendez		**Base hourly rate:**		$15.00
	Actual Hours	**Adjusted Hours**		**Amount**
Normal time			$	
Time and a half		(x1.5)	$	
Double Time		(x2)	$	
Triple time		(x3)	$	
Personal Leave			$	
Annual Leave			$	
Leave Loading 17.5%			$	
Less Salary Sacrifice			$	
GROSS PAY			$	
DEDUCTIONS				
PAYG TAX	$			
LESS Rebate	$			
NET Tax deducted		$		
Additional Super		$		
Savings Plan		$		
Trade Union		$		
Health Insurance		$		
TOTAL DEDUCTIONS			$	
NET PAY			$	

Pay Slip	
Elite Co. ABN 11 111 111 111	
Name:	Jo Mendez
Pay Ending:	08/03/CY
Normal Wage	
Overtime	
Personal/Holiday	
Less Sal Sacrifice	
GROSS PAY	
Deductions	
Tax	
Additional Super	
Savings	
Union	
Health	
Total Deductions	
Net Pay	
Super Fund	Spectrum Super
Super Amount	

Scenario 6.2 (continued)

Elite Co.

ELITE CO				
PAYROLL SUMMARY			**Pay ending:**	8/3/CY
Wages	HOLMES Janet	MENDEZ Jo	TOTALS	Date Paid
Normal				
Overtime 1.5x				
Overtime 2x				
Overtime 3x				
Annual Leave				
Personal Leave				
GROSS PAY				
Less Sal Sac				
ADJ GROSS PAY				
DEDUCTIONS				
Net Tax				
Additional Super				
Savings Plan				
Trade Union				
Health Insurance				
TOTAL DEDUCTIONS				
NET PAY				
Super Guarantee				
Total Super				

Authorised:		Date:
Processed:		Date:

General Journal					GJ4
Date	Particulars		Folio	Debit	Credit

Exercise 6.3

Abel Co.

Abel Co. Holiday Pay Calculation Card		No. of Weeks:	4
Name: Liz Toll		Base Hourly Rate:	$15.00
Leave Commenced: 14/3/CY		Leave Finished: 10/04/CY	
Weekly Holiday Pay	$		
less Salary Sacrifice	$		
Plus 17.5% Leave Loading	$		
WEEKLY HOLIDAY PAY	$		
Weeks paid in advance			
GROSS PAY		$	
DEDUCTIONS			
Calculate Income Tax			
Tax on weekly holiday pay less rebate	$		
Times Weeks paid in advance		4	
Total holiday tax	$		
DEDUCTIONS times weeks of leave	$		
Additional Super $ times 4 weeks	$		
Savings Plan $10 times 4 weeks	$		
Trade Union $5 times 4 weeks	$		
Health Insurance $18 times 4 weeks	$		
TOTAL DEDUCTIONS		$	
NET PAY		$	

Scenario 6.3

Elite Co.

Elite Co. Wages Calculation Card		F/night End: 22/3/CY	
Name: Janet Holmes		**Base hourly rate:** $18.00	
	Actual Hours	**Adjusted Hours**	**Amount**
Normal time			
Time and a half		(x1.5)	
Double Time		(x2)	
Triple time		(x3)	
Personal Leave			$
Annual Leave			$
Leave Loading 17.5%			$
Less Salary Sacrifice			$
GROSS PAY			$
DEDUCTIONS			
PAYG TAX	$		
LESS Rebate	$		
NET Tax deducted		$	
Additional Super		$	
Savings Plan		$	
Trade Union		$	
Health Insurance		$	
TOTAL DEDUCTIONS			$
NET PAY			$

Pay Slip	
Elite Co. ABN 11 111 111 111	
Name:	Janet Holmes
Pay Ending:	22/3/CY
Normal Wage	
Overtime	
Personal/Holiday	
Less Sal Sacrifice	
GROSS PAY	
Deductions	
Tax	
Additional Super	
Savings	
Union	
Health	
Total Deductions	
Net Pay	
Super Fund	Spectrum Super
Super Amount	

Elite Co. Holiday Pay Calculation Card		No. of Weeks: 4	
Name: Jo Mendez		**Base Hourly Rate:** $15.00	
Leave Commenced:		Leave Finished:	
Weekly Holiday Pay	$		
less Salary Sacrifice	$		
Plus 17.5% Leave Loading	$		
WEEKLY HOLIDAY PAY	$		
Weeks paid in advance			
GROSS PAY		$	
DEDUCTIONS			
Calculate Income Tax			
Tax on weekly holiday pay less rebate	$		
Times Weeks paid in advance			
Total holiday tax	$		
DEDUCTIONS times weeks of leave	$		
Additional Super $ times 4 weeks	$		
Savings Plan $10 times 4 weeks	$		
Trade Union $5 times 4 weeks	$		
Health Insurance $18 times 4 weeks	$		
TOTAL DEDUCTIONS		$	
NET PAY		$	

Scenario 6.3 (continued)

Elite Co.

Pay Slip	
Elite Co. ABN 11 111 111 111	
Name:	Jo Mendez
Pay Ending:	22/3/CY
Normal Wage	
Overtime	
Personal/Holiday	
Less Sal Sacrifice	
GROSS PAY	
Deductions	
Tax	
Additional Super	
Savings	
Union	
Health	
Total Deductions	
Net Pay	
Super Fund	Spectrum Super
Super Amount	

ELITE CO				
PAYROLL SUMMARY			**Pay ending:**	22/3/CY
Wages	HOLMES Janet	MENDEZ Jo	TOTALS	Date Paid
Normal				
Overtime 1.5x				
Overtime 2x				
Overtime 3x				
Annual Leave				
Personal Leave				
GROSS PAY				
Less Sal Sac				
ADJ GROSS PAY				
DEDUCTIONS				
Net Tax				
Additional super				
Savings Plan				
trade union				
Health Insurance				
TOTAL DEDUCTIONS				
NET PAY				
Super Guarantee				
Total Super				
Authorised:			Date:	
Processed:			Date:	

Scenario 6.3 (continued)

Elite Co.

General Journal				GJ4
Date	Particulars	Folio	Debit	Credit

Scenario 7.1

Elite Co. Sales GST

BAS	JOURNAL	Excl GST	GST Collctd	Totals
	ELITE CO			
	1 JANUARY TO 31 MARCH 20CY			
	INFORMATION WORKSHEET - CASH BASIS			
	Cash Receipts (Cash Sales with GST)			
G2	Cash Receipts (cash export sales)			
G3	Cash Receipts (GST Free)			
	Cash Receipts (from debtors)			
G4	Cash receipts (input tax)			
G3	General Journal - Receipts			
G7	Adjustments			
	TOTALS			
	BAS LABELS		1A	G1

							Cash Receipts Journal					CR1
Date	Rcpt	Particulars	Folio	Discnt	GST Adj	Acct Rec	Sales	GST Collctd	General	Bank
4/3	025	Cash Sale	4.11				1,122.00	112.20		1,234.20
18/3	026	Cash Sale	4.12					700.00	7,000.00	7,700.00
21/3	027	Y Yao	C 03	35.00	3.50	731.50				
21/3	028	Touma P/L	C 01			2,200.00				2,931.50
28/3	029	Interest Income	8.1						32.00	32.00
31/3	030	Y Yao	C 03			1,430.00				
31/3	031	V Maris	C 02			550.00				1,980.00
				35.00	3.50	4,911.50	1,122.00	812.20	7,032.00	13,877.70
				Cr 1.12	Cr 1.12	Dr 2.131	Dr 2.131	Cr 2.131	Cr 4.12/8.1	Cr 1.10
				Cr 5.9	Dr 2.131					

	General Journal			GJ1
Date	Particulars	Folio	Debit	Credit
31/3	Cheque Account	1.10	1,320.00	
	Furniture & Fixtures at Cost	1.311		1,200.00
	GST Collected	2.131		120.00
	Sale of old jewellers desk			
31/3	Accounts Receivable	1.12	1,650.00	
	Jewellery Evaluation	4.12		1,500.00
	GST Collected	2.131		150.00
	Sales Invoice 115 (V Maris)			

Scenario 7.1

Elite Co. Purchases GST

	ELITE CO 1 JANUARY TO 31 MARCH 20CY INFORMATION WORKSHEET - CASH BASIS			
Work sheet	Journal	Excl GST	GST Paid	Totals
	General Journal (Cash Assets Purchase)			
	Cash Payments (Asset Purchase)			
	TOTALS			
	WORKSHEET LABELS		G20	G10
	Cash Payments (expenses with GST)			
	Cash Payments (to creditors)			
G13	Cash Payments (purchases for making input taxed sales)			
G14	Purchases (No ABN)			
	General Journal (Cash purchases with GST)			
G14	Cash Payments (Interest)			
G18	ADJUSTMENTS			
	TOTALS			
	BAS LABELS		G20	G11

	Cash Payments Journal									CP1
Date	Rcpt	Particulars	Folio	Discnt	GST Adj	Acct Rec	Sales	GST Collctd	General	Bank
15/3	0015	Cheok & Son	S 03			5,148.00				5,148.00
26/3	0016	Bui & Co	S 01	170.00	17.00	3,553.00				3,553.00
30/3	017	Officeworks	6.18					14.20	142.00	156.00
31/3	018	Kalgoorlie Mint	5.12				5,000.00	500.00		5,500.00
				170.00	17.00	8,701.00	5,000.00	514.20	142.00	14,357.00

	General Journal			GJ1
Date	Particulars	Folio	Debit	Credit
31/3	Furniture and Fixtures at Cost	1.311	4,000.00	
	GST Paid	2.132	400.00	
	Bank Loan	2.20		4,400.00
	Purchase new display cabinet			
31/3	Maintenance	6.17	1,600.00	
	GST Paid	2.132	160.00	
	Accounts Payable	2.12		1,760.00
	Purchase Invoice 1091 (V Maris)			
31/3	Accounts Payable	2.12	1,650.00	
	Accounts Receivable	1.12		1,650.00
	Contra Deal with V Maris			

This is the Contra Deal. Even though the supplier invoice was for $1,760, only $1,650 was offset in the contra deal. There is still $110 left to pay.

Scenario 7.1

Elite Co. BAS

Goods and Services tax (GST)
For the quarter from 1 Jan 2016 to 31 Mar 2016

Complete the marked cells

☑ Option 1: Calculate GST and report quarterly

PAYG Tax Withheld

Total Sales	G1	$	

Does the amount at G1 include GST?
(indicate with a x)   ☑ Yes ☐ No

Export Sales	G2	$	
Other GST-Free sales	G3	$	
Capital purchases	G10	$	
Non-capital Purchases	G11	$	

Go to summary over the page to report GST on sales at 1A and GST on purchases at 1B

PAYG Tax Withheld

Total Salary, wages and other payments	W1	$	
Amounts Withheld from payments shown at W1	W2	$	
Amounts withheld where no ABN is quoted	W4	$	
Other amounts withheld (excluding any amount shown at	W3	$	
Total Amounts withheld (W2+W3+W4)	W5	$	

Write at 4 in summary below

PAYG Income Tax Instalment

☑ Option 2: Calculate PAYG instalment using income x rate

PAYG Instalment Income	T1	$	
Commissioner's rate	T2		%
OR			
New Varied Rate	T3		%
T1 x T2 (or x T3)	T11	$	

Continued over page...

Scenario 7.2
Elite Co. BAS

Goods and Services tax (GST)
For the quarter from 1 Jan 2016 to 31 Mar 2016

Complete the marked cells

Summary
Amounts you owe the ATO

GST on Sales or GST Instalment	**1A**	$
PAYG tax withheld	**4**	$
PAYG income tax instalment	**5A**	$
eferred company/fund instalment	**7**	$
1A + 4 + 5A + 7	**8A**	$

Amounts the ATO owes you

GST on purchases	**1B**	$

Do not complete if using GST instalment amount (Option 3)

Credit from PAYG income tax instalment variation	**5B**	$
1B + 5B	**8A**	$

Payment or refund?   ☑ Yes

Write the result of 8A minus 8B at 9. This amount is payable to the ATO.

9 $

Write the result of 8A minus 8B at 9. This amount is refundable to you (or offset against any other tax debt you have)

Do not use symbols such as +,-,/,$

Is 8A more than 8B?   ☐ No
(indicate with an x)

Scenario 7.3

Elite Co.

	General Journal			GJ1
Date	Particulars	Folio	Debit	Credit